MW00475682

# THE GREAT TOMORROW

# THE GREAT TOMORROW

### BY
### NICK BUNICK

Also by Nick Bunick

*The Messengers*

*In God's Truth*

*Transitions of the Soul*

*The Commitment*

*Time for Truth*

(Description of each book located in the back of this book)

# CONTENTS

Copyright © 2013 by Nick Bunick

**Published and distributed in the United States by:** Nick Bunick.: www.nickbunick.com •

*Design cover:   Miyana Brkic*          *Editorial Supervision: Miryana Brkic*

All rights reserved. No part of this book may be reproduced by any mechanical, photographic, or electronic process, or in the form of a phonographic recording; nor may it be stored in a retrieval system, transmitted, or otherwise be copied for public or private use—other than for "fair use" as brief quotations embodied in articles and reviews—without prior written permission of the publisher.

The author of this book does not dispense medical advice or prescribe the use of any technique as a form of treatment for physical, emotional, or medical problems without the advice of a physician, either directly or indirectly. The intent of the author is only to offer information of a general nature to help you in your quest for emotional and spiritual well-being. In the event you use any of the information in this book for yourself, which is your constitutional right, the author and the publisher assume no responsibility for your actions.

**Library of Congress Cataloging-in-Publication Data**

Bunick, Nick.
 The Great Tomorrow / Nick Bunick. -- 1st ed.
    p. cm.

   ISBN-13:978-1494710743

   ISBN-10:1494710749

(tradepaper : alk. paper) 1. Spiritual, Inspirational, Religion. 2. Bunick, Nick.


1st edition, December 2013

# Forward

It is has been written and said many times, do not judge a book by its cover. I also want to share with you, do not judge a book by its size.

A few years ago the information contained within this book *The Great Tomorrow* was made available to me by my spiritual sources. At that time, I did not have the ability or the needed spiritual evolvement to decipher it completely... and put it into words that could be understood by others.

As I continued to evolve on my own spiritual journey, the clouds were lifted and clarity was made available to me. Not only did I begin to comprehend the information that was being provided to me...I found that I could now process it from my own conscious mind, and put into words that hopefully most people would understand, in the written word.

Unlike my other five books, *The Messengers, In God's Truth, Transitions of the Soul, Time for Truth* and *The Commitment,* I recognize and acknowledge that this book, *The Great Tomorrow*, may not be understood by everyone.

When I refer to my other five published books as being understood, I am not suggesting that they were accepted by everyone. There have been postings on my website, nickbunick.com from some that have rejected what was contained in the other five books..

Then there was the time my website was literally attacked by hackers so severely, that it was taken out of operation for a few days. But this was not the result of their not understanding what I had written, but rather in dispute of the words of truth that were contained in these five books.

*The Great Tomorrow* is different but surely it will be a very controversial book. It will probably have the same critics and dissenters that I have had in the past. But this time, it will have gone one step further, in that many of the critics will not understand what has been written within these pages.

I have no sympathy towards them, for those who do not seek the truth, or recognize truth when it is provided to them. My concern is for those who indeed do seek the truth, and want to evolve to higher levels in their desire to become at one with God and Christ Consciousness. But I am concerned that the words within this book may be beyond their comprehension.

If you do understand the wisdom and revelation contained within, then you are one of those this book indeed was meant for you to read. However, the other issue, do you not only understand the words within, but do you identify with them? That is between you and your soul mind. If you do not understand that you indeed have a soul mind, then you are really in an unfavorable position, for then how would you even be able to receive my information and process it in accordance with spirit's will?

Back to the size of this book. I deliberately kept it short for there is so much to absorb and to try to understand. I was not seeking a Best Seller based on its length. Otherwise I could have fed you the pablum that is put out by some authors that assume to have a book be a Best Seller it must have pages after pages of material that mainly benefits those who manufacture paper and the publishing companies who charge the readers more money if the book does have more pages. You will find this is 100% accurate. Ask any honest author.

So this book, *The Great Tomorrow*, is to be Volume One. Will there be a volume Two? You are the ones that will make that decision. It is your response to *The Great Tomorrow* that will determine if I share with you the rest of the information that I have been provided, as well as continue to receive data from the spiritual world to my soul mind, and which then becomes shared with you in future volumes of The Great Tomorrow. For if there are no readers, why should there be an author?

How many potential volumes are there? I do not know. it will depend on how many future years as a mortal that my spirit/soul continues in this form. As I have said and have written many times, "We are not human beings that by coincidence have a spirit an a soul. We are spirits with a soul that are having a human experience."

Some day I will also be in spirit and my soul will be in another dimension, as yours will some day also,..and perhaps at that time I will be a spirit/soul that is sending this information to another spirit/soul that is in a mortal body, so I become the one sending the channeled messages rather than the one receiving the channeling..

Then *The Great Tomorrow* could have infinite volumes, which would then be read by your great grandchildren, and their children. But if they start with Volume One, it may take them their entire lifetime to read all the volumes, as new ones continue to be channeled and written by the mortal soul that would now have that task, the same one that I now have, as I write these words.

Have I lost you yet? Should I make it more interesting....or confusing? Then I am reincarnated, am born again, 100 years from now..and I am once again reading my own Volume One, and receiving new material to make into future volumes.

Will you understand what I am sharing... by the time you finish reading this book *The Great Tomorrow*? We will soon find out, won't we?.

At any rate, this FORWARD is long enough...or this book will also become one with too many pages..for I could write a volume on just the issues I have raised in this FORWARD.

You are about to go on a journey that will change your life forever..or you may never get past the first chapter. We will soon discover whether this book was written for you or not.

But either way, God bless you as you continue on your journey.

Nick Bunick

## Chapter One

# The Teachings

We are not human beings that by coincidence have a spirit and soul. We are spirits with a soul that are having a human experience. Our spirit is that part of us that comes from God. We have a part of God's spirit within us, which is why we are eternal and immortal.

Our soul is the intellect of our spirit, the personality of our spirit; our soul determines our spirit's values, its beliefs, and it is constantly changing with every experience we have in every one of our lifetimes. Yes, we experience many lifetimes, which I shall provide you with proof from the teachings I will share with you.

The origin of the philosophies that I am going to share with you, the thoughts and teachings cannot easily be understood by the average human mind. I am bringing these beliefs to you that originated from times long gone. These principles date back prior to recognized historical times; as far back as forgotten Lemuria, that few people actually believe existed. Then onward to ancient Atlantis that most still consider as a myth, civilizations that historians and scientists do not accept as reality.

I am beginning with a very controversial position, and I will continue in dealing with concepts which to many may create distrust, resistance and rejection, yet concepts that I know to be truth. The average person has difficulty dealing with esoteric thoughts. They find them new and strange to them, and a challenge to their minds. Most people will find it farfetched to accept these extraordinary principles that I am going to share with you, rather than consider them carefully and open minded.

So these thoughts are being offered to those who are prepared to think for themselves, and who are willing to explore and delve deeper into these aspects of life which are not readily obvious, concepts which are not in conformance with the accepted physical and emotional patterns of their daily lives.

As far as life is concerned, some people today do at times reflect on the inner hidden meaning of life, even if it is only to meditate momentarily on subject matters such as the real significance of death…and whether there may perhaps be some truth that death may not be an absolute and the finality, the end of life, that there may remain some form of continued spiritual existence after separating with the physical body, that there is a transition of our soul to the spiritual world when our body no longer is a part of. I refer to this as a transition of our souls which I have written about in my previous books.

Even those who lead normal lives, occasionally consider there may be entirely different possibilities as to the existence, the influence and the nature of the spiritual realms. On one side is the one extreme, those who, In public, will argue passionately against the possibility of any spiritual existence. But on the other hand there are also many who are sincere believers in the continuity of life and that human destiny is guided by unknown powers in another dimension of some nature.

There are also those who are very much in tune with and aware of guidance from higher levels, who identify themselves with having souls and having a part of God's spirit within them as I have stated earlier. Some speak of a divine power called God who is responsible for the Universe.

At any rate, theses concepts vary in extreme wide ranges, and if these views were analyzed carefully, it is doubtful that any two individuals would have the exact same ideas as to the details of their religious beliefs, or their understanding of the unknown world of spirit.

To many of the religious people, their religion is most often purely emotional or devotional, which they do not want to have challenged. In most cases they have been taught religious dogmas since they were a child. The result is that most people have bought into the habit of blindly accepting those beliefs, and it never seems to occur to them to question these credos and give them deeper consideration.

Often these individuals do not want to subject their beliefs to deep thought, for perhaps deep within them there indeed may be a feeling of doubt and uncertainty. They are not prepared to subject their beliefs to logic because they are afraid that the religious support on which they have been relying on since early youth, may be swept away from under their feet, that the religious belief may be built on a foundation of jello, rather than stone.

The ancient wisdom that I will share with you should not be considered a religion. However some of these principles will become part of future religious beliefs. But for now, we shall think of them as a philosophy, an effort to understand the relationship between humanity and the rest of the Universe of which humankind is a very minute but nonetheless intimate part of. The teachings that I will offer are intended to help you arrive at a better realization of humanity's own nature and basic constitution.

How is humanity related to the spiritual aspects of life; of the role humanity has played in the past and is destined to play in the future? I will make an effort to describe and define energy. What are its functions? To what extent can it be controlled or affected by the human being? So it will be a study of the interrelationship of humanity with all that constitutes our world...and what is the effect of the energies and the forces as a result of this contact. This evaluation of these aspects and points of views and its acceptance will depend on the level of understanding of each individual person that is receiving this information.

If I were to tell you that the concept of hell was adopted by Church leaders in the fourth century from a dump that burned twenty-four hours a day 2000 years ago outside of Jerusalem in the Valley of Hinnon, would you believe me? The dump was called Gehenna in Hebrew, which means hell in English. That is where the concept of hell came from. That is truth, although I know some of you may resist in accepting that truth.

So, as I have already mentioned, although this information cannot be considered as being religion, these concepts may indeed lead to a new religious practice. But as a matter of fact, all of the hundreds of religions and religious beliefs which exist today throughout the world, are in reality founded on the basic principles of the ageless wisdom. The principles and truths that have been interpreted, adapted and preached by various prophets, messengers, teachers, and seers over the ages were done so to meet the needs of specific groups of people under their own particular circumstances.

Although these teachings originated from the same fundamental source, many of these teachings have been distorted beyond recognition today. Sometimes this happened as a result of faulty interpretation, so that incorrect information has been handed down from generation to generation, and in other instances it was the result of deliberate falsification of the truth to suit the selfish objectives of individuals seeking power.

I am confident that every person will have their own interpretation of what I will be sharing, and that interpretation will vary depending on each person's own experiences and knowledge of spirituality. As to how much each individual will benefit from this information will depend on their own level of spiritual development and their own "soul's knowledge.

As I stated earlier, every one of us has a spirit and soul and our spirit is that part of God's spirit that is within each of us. We are eternal and immortal because we do have a part of God's spirit within us. …..And worth repeating, our soul is the intellect, the personality, possesses the values, and the knowledge we express as a result of all of its experiences in every lifetime we have had. Again, you must understand, we are not human beings that happen to have a spirit and a soul. We are spirits with soul that are having a human experience.

For me to state that the origin of the teachings go back thousands and even much further into the past is true and yet has to be characterized. The teachings were certainly taught and passed on in those times gone by, but they were much simpler and easier to put into practice than they would be today. They could be more comparable to the level of our educating our children today. The wisdom in the teachings in their original form was derived from some divine Source beyond human understanding. Although the teachings basically remain unchanged, they are nevertheless modified from age to age, and from civilization to civilization. This was done to meet the needs of that particular age and that environment, and also to match the mental development of humanity in each particular era.

During Lemurian times for instance, humanity was mainly physically oriented. Their main concerns were concentrated on the feeding of the people and protecting themselves. They were not inclined to be emotional in nature, but gradually the emotions began to awaken but that was eons of years later, during the Atlantean age.

It was at that time that emotional life started to play a more important role and eventually came to dominate physical stimulus. But it was only during the present age, the Aryan age that the mind obtained a stronger hold on humanity. But even now, there is a need for many more people to evolve spiritually to a higher level.

I want you to visualize inside of each of you, a pyramid of a thousand steps. At the very top of the pyramid is God and Christ Consciousness. And your goal is to climb as many of the stairs as possible, evolving, to become closer and closer until you reach the top and become at one with God and Christ Consciousness, no matter how many lifetimes it takes.

But in today's world, there are so few people near the top. History shows you which ones reached the top, those who gave so much to society and were committed in making our world a better one to live in. They sacrificed, they fought for truth, they were criticized and condemned, and ridiculed many times, even crucified, but their accomplishments endured and they made a difference in the world. And we also recognize those who were at the bottom of the pyramid, at steps five and six, the Hitlers in the world, the Stalins and Bin Ladens They also influenced humanity, and led nations and people into a collective evil consciousness.

Sadly today, the average step on the pyramid for the majority of the people in the world is at 200. Most people are still dominated by their egos, with the spiritual part of their being playing a secondary function. Why are there hungry children in the world, although we as a world society are capable of feeding every child in the world? Why are billions spent on products of war, offensive and defensive weapons, rather than those being funds and resources spent to care for the sick and the poor? Why aren't the people of the world and our leaders living their lives embracing universal love and universal compassion?

It stands to reason that the teachings presented to the Lemurians as well as those of Atlantea, though based on the same principals of spiritual truth, could not possibly have been cast in the mould as is required today. The teachings needed to be understood today would be incomprehensible to the epicurean Lemurians as well as to even the most advanced Atlanteans.

Humanity today has access to the scriptures and teaching of prophets of the past, those who were responsible for passing the teachings onward. As humanity developed and became more receptive to the Divine Truths, they were bound to be provided from one source to another. Consciously or unconsciously humanity were provided the teachings when they were ready to receive them and were in need of them. The teachings would inevitably reach them, and at the same time would try to clarify and amplify much of the deeper and hidden messages.... understandings which previously either escaped humanity's notice or were obscure to most of the world.

Although Buddha, Christ, Mohammed and some of the other Masters may be quoted as the direct source of certain teachings, it should always be understood that these loved and revered Teachers were in reality channels for the transmissions of the Divine Truths which originated from Higher Divine sources. These teachings would be totally incomprehensible to humanity if they were received in their originating purity, so they are stepped down from one spiritual level to the lower ones in more simplified forms.

As these teachings are brought down to lower dimensions they finally are provided on the physical plane through human speech or the written word. Through this process some of its spiritual qualities had to be sacrificed, thereby reducing their original meanings being conveyed. Also the distortions of the teachings by those in power may have become so severe that the original teachings could hardly be recognized. This has happened in the teachings of Christ, as they were drastically distorted by those in power in the fourth century that formulated the beginning of organized Christianity.

Under the new founded church at that time, which is now known as the Roman Catholic Church, the leaders so distorted the teachings, so that messages  of love became messages of fear, messages of compassion became messages of guilt, and message that were intended to bring humanity together, instead were formulated to do just the opposite, and polarized humanity.

These distortions have *caused* great harm over the last sixteen hundred years, and those who are followers of this religion are now in need to be provided the "truth". If they are not, the Church will not survive and other new organized religions will spring forth to replace the role that the Church represented. I have written about these distortions in great detail in my previous books, The Messengers, Time for Truth and The Commitment. Many would choose in having a relationship with the Divinity through a spiritual bond rather than through an organized religion.

One of the most important needs of those seeking the Path of Truth, is to strive toward an ever expanding spiritual consciousness, in order to obtain the purest understanding of the teachings, so they can share this knowledge with others. This occurs as one ascends the steps of their pyramid I wrote of earlier, evolving closer to becoming at one with God and Christ Consciousness.

It must be understood that no one is ever provided deeper spiritual knowledge for their own purely personal or selfish benefit. Let us next examine the role religion has played in our lives and will in the future.

## Chapter Two

# Religion

Religion is the relationship with society with their subjective worlds. It concerns how people approach the understanding for God in their search for guidance and support in their daily lives and how to respond to life's challenges and stress.

Calling upon the aid of a Divine Source is always more prevalent during times of great difficulty and dealing with anguish and despair in one's life. Fortunately people will soon realize there is a Divine Source that can provide relief for their wounded hearts and minds.

The ancient teachings indicate the broad principles and laws underlying religion. They indicate humanity's relationship to the Source, and the way humanity should act and live to make contact with, and to receive the energies and spiritual support from the one they refer to as God, instead of trying to be self-sufficient. If humanity could achieve having a clear and true understanding of their relationship with God, then humanity would recognize the physical impossibility of an existence without God in their lives.

Sometimes when people achieve power and wealth without God in their lives, this often is acquired and accompanied with misery and disenchantment. It is so true that money cannot buy happiness. Joy, in reality, is something intangible, and of the spirit, and can only be attained by being in harmony with that part of God inside of us. We are part of God and God is part of us. Our goal in life is to become at one with that part of God inside of us. You cannot do this until you reach a certain level, achieve a certain step on your

13

pyramid as you try to evolve spiritually, in your goal to become at one with God and Christ Consciousness.

The ancient Teachings however, are not to be thought of as a religion. They are instead, a philosophy, a search for truth, a serious study and consideration of the underlying forces affecting and controlling our lives, and relating humanity to the rest of the Universe. All religions are based on the same fundamental concepts as the Teachings, but instead of allowing man's mind free play in its ever expanding search for truth, religious leaders and theologians have been attempting to control their followers to dogmatic and distorted doctrines and messages, mostly for the purpose of having power and influence over their followers.

Whether a person today belongs to a religion or not, it is largely determined by that person's family, community or religion the person was born into. Most religions differ very little from one another, and the existing differences are man-made, and do not encompass the interpretations of the Truth, but instead are various dogmas and rituals, which were originated by humans.

The world is passing through a temporary state of chaos in many aspects, as it relates to religion. People are beginning to revolt against the traditional power, authority and domination by these religious leaders and doctrines that have been wielding power for centuries. The result is that people are beginning to question and reject the traditional authority of these old institutions.

As I described in my book *Time for Truth*, in Italy, where 97 percent of the population is Catholic, only 30 percent of these people attend church. In France, where 76 percent of the population is Catholic, only 12 percent attend church. And in Germany, only 13 percent of the Catholics attend church. In my country, the USA, only 32 percent of Catholics attend church.

Many concepts are no longer being accepted. I mentioned earlier, that two thousand years ago there was a dump outside of Jerusalem in the Valley of Hinnen that burned twenty-four hours a day, called Gehenna. Gehenna means hell in English and in the fourth century, when the Church was founded, this is when the Church leaders adopted the concept of hell.

And in the year 2000 when Pope John Paul announced in a Vatican speech that the Church should stop preaching a hell, for hell is the state of a person's mind when a person is living outside of the

God's will, but those who manage and control the Vatican and the Church insisted they maintain the concept of hell so that sinners will continue to live in fear.

People are tired of the discrimination against women in the Church. The Church claims that Jesus had twelve disciples but they do not tell you that the word disciples comes from the ancient Greek word discipulous which means pupils. Did Jesus really have only twelve pupils? Jesus had hundreds of pupils, disciples, and half of them were women. And when the Apostle Paul traveled throughout the Roman Empire creating his churches, half of the administrators he appointed were women.

But when Paul wrote about these women in the 4th century when the Church made his letters public, they changed the women's names to men's names....Indeed, it is time for the Church to allow women to become priests and hold positions of responsibility with the church.

Another major change that should be made by the Church is to allow priests to be married and have families. The Apostle Paul never intended to confine priesthoods to only men who were not married. He never required that his priests be celibate. This requirement on the part of the Church has had a devastating effect on the Church for many years, including pedophile activities and have denied hundreds of thousands of able and qualified men and women to become dedicated members of the clergy.

The origin and history of religions and the foundation of the doctrines are now being deeply investigated, including many of the old established concepts to the nature of man, man's destiny and man's soul, as well as the nature of Divinity. They are being reconsidered and even rejected. This will lead to endless disputes, confusion and uncertainty, and new schools of thought will be formed. From these medley of thoughts, ideas, speculations and theories, will emerge new churches, religions and sects.

In reality, there will still be those clinging to their traditional religious beliefs, who do not want to see any changes. They usually belong to the older generation, and prefer that there be obedience to the established theological or religious authority. This group is often recognized by their devotional attitude, which often includes positions of intolerance.

Their beliefs are often distorted being biased by dogmatic concepts and not by logical reason by an enlightened mind. The divine intelligence which they have been given by God has been cast aside and they are unable to adapt themselves to the progressively unfolding world of new ideas, new visions and spiritual development. But the standards they maintain in common with their Church teachings are doomed to eventual extinction.

I am reminded of the time I was flying on a flight and next to me at the window seat was a young woman reading the New Testament. Coincidently enough, she was reading one of Paul's letters, one that my spirit and soul wrote through Paul 2,000 years ago. I began a conversation with her and found her to very pleasant and personable. She shared with me that she had married a Jewish man but had persuaded him to convert to her religion so he would not go to hell when he died. Then she volunteered that she felt a great sadness for his parents, who had not converted. She said they were wonderful people and how sad it was that they would go to hell when they died.

I tried to gently reason with her, but it was obvious to me as described above, her beliefs were ingrained in her and I could sense she was beginning to get uncomfortable in trying to defend her illogical reasoning. But there are some people, although not yet large in numbers, who have revolted against the religious establishment. Among them are idealists, and potential thinkers who may join together and enlarge the ranks of another group that might be labeled as intellectual mystics who are deeply spiritually oriented.

These people are intellectually focused and not acting from an emotional motivation. They do not belong to any organized group or to a specific race, creed or color. Their only bond is that they speak the same spiritual language, a language that consists of the same nucleus of beliefs, without these beliefs being dogmatic. They also recognize the role played by new spiritual leaders in the world who are shaping the foundations of these spiritual understandings.

The group described above may be regarded as the nucleus of the coming spiritual revolution which will finally encompass the people of the whole world into a single spiritual world society, The Great Tomorrow. There will be a meaningful spiritual awakening that will be happening throughout the world, with an urgent need for Truth. Humanity will have never before been so spiritually hungry, in need of spiritual values and a true understanding of their relationship with God. People will not only be searching for Light, but where to find it.

Orthodox church leaders certainly do not provide that Light. They are either limited by their narrow theological interpretations of the Scriptures, which the masses are no longer prepared to accept or have abandoned religion and are content to be committed to a material life without God being a part of it.

Those with Christian backgrounds no longer want to be told they were born condemned by God to go to hell when they die because a woman (Eve) in a garden was told by a snake to persuade her husband (Adam) to take a bite out of an apple that God had forbidden them to do, thereby creating Original Sin....but that they could be saved if they allowed themselves to be baptized..... but everybody else in the world otherwise would surely go to hell. They no longer want to be told Jeshua (Jesus) died because they are sinners and he was crucified so they could be forgiven for their sins.

In the past all religions have produced ambitious people who were thinkers and leaders who formulated their own ideas as to what is God and the meaning of their scriptures into doctrines and dogmas that then became accepted by those seeking religion and foisted on the unthinking and needy who became their faithful followers.

But during this coming time of history, many will challenge these dogmas and doctrines, for they will be no longer satisfied with being dictated to as to what they should believe or not believe....they want to reason things out themselves and reach their own conclusions. They want freedom in all respects, including how to interpret their relationship with God and their purpose in life.

These explorers of **freedom of the mind** want to be provided with the facts and the truths as being offered in these Teachings, but it must be left for them to decide what they wish to incorporate into their spiritual beliefs. Provided these explorers are honestly and sincerely motivated, their spiritual enfoldment is assured and will become a reality. Humanity can never be saved by theological dogmas, but only by awakening and becoming at one with that part of God inside of each and every one of us.

I have shared with you the devastating and failing affects that the narrow outlook of many church leaders have had on their followers. Many of these church leaders are well meaning people who are doing their best in accordance with what they have been taught and the tools they have to work with. In the ministry of their church duties they have been teaching dogmatic tenets instead of sharing the true spirit of Christ Consciousness.

If these Church preachers could only become men of God in the true sense, rather than church-men, and allow themselves to connect with and teach the true messages of God and Christ Consciousness, then they could then become the spiritual leaders of the future.

These same people would then realize and acknowledge that there is only One Religion and only One Church , God's Church. And that same God should be the foundation of every faith, every race and color of mankind, and that the fullness of the Truth will only be realized through God's Church and God's Religion; that mankind is made up of all God's children, and in reality, we are all brothers and sisters,

When I traveled throughout the United States in 1987 speaking in front of large audiences after my New York Times best seller, *The Messengers*, was published, I was often asked the question what religion I was. I always answered that I was the same religion that God is. The questioner would look at me puzzled and then ask, "What religion is God?" And I would answer, that God does not have a religion. Well, it is **time** for the establishment of God's Religion.

All nations, with their many religions, have one bond in common, and that is their belief in a Supreme Being. Their deity is called by many names and honored by many different ceremonies and rituals, with the masses being unaware of the fact that in all these instances they are actually paying homage to the same entity.

Once all people of the world arrive at the recognition that they have one common God, it will also bring the realization that we are indeed all brothers and sisters, one great family, one humanity. Out of this recognition will then be born God's Church and God's Religion which will unite men and women all over the world into one spiritual and loving family, truly embracing universal love and universal compassion for everybody.

The world will soon be coming under the influence of the new spiritual energy and emerge out of the present chaos that presently exists. A new spirituality will gradually be imposed on the present disorganized and splintered condition of religious worship, and this will step by step lead to new social orders and worldwide relationships among all people.

These changes will become expressed in all fronts of human activity... social, economic, scientific, political as well as spiritual. It is out of the present religious turbulence that God's religion will evolve. These great changes will indeed take time, but will come sooner than would generally be expected.

The devotional approach of God's religion will also be intellectually oriented, and will be influenced also by those of the scientific world who will want to prove to their followers the Path of Truth. Their present skepticism will fade away, and then the concern will arise that this intellectual approach might become dominant; that the devotional and the mystic aspects might be pushed into the background, thus causing confrontations and lack of unity.

Concepts of the Truth should always be evolving and never come to a conclusion. In addition to the mental and intellectual awakening, a corresponding spiritual understanding will also take its natural course, with humanity constantly searching for fresh interpretations of the Teachings and its spiritual principles. Humanity will never again be satisfied with being told what to believe or what to reject, for humanity will be searching for Truth, and in finding Truth, humanity will become aware of the personal relationship with our Creator. This can and will be achieved without the mediation and the authority of a church, the dogmatic creeds of priests or dogmatic rituals.

Once men and women become conscious of their own soul and that they have within them the spirit of God, no imposed religion in the future will be able to block or restrain this spiritual development that will ensue, in humanity striving and evolving to become at one with God and Christ Consciousness.

Spiritual minded people of the future will largely be guided by these underlying attitudes towards religion. The future religious teachings will be spiritually oriented and will not be governed by dogmatic doctrines, but on principles, which may be summarized as:

(a) Spiritual Freedom, and therefore freedom of thought and choice, each person having to work out their own understanding how to evolve spiritually, how to climb the steps of their pyramid in their commitment to become at one with God and Christ Consciousness.

(b) Spiritual love towards humanity, which means living their lives embracing universal love and universal compassion, expressed by selfless sharing and mutual caring for one another.

All religion will then be regarded as emanating from One single spiritual Source, and this will gradually draw humanity together to be united in understanding that we are all brothers and sisters, children of God.

This does not mean there would be a single homogeneous group in which all races are then physically, socially and politically the same. On the contrary, the beauty of this becoming a reality would lie in many differences in the different races, skin colors, ethnics, languages, histories and cultures, but still bound together by common spiritual principles and common understandings of their relationship with God and the purpose of life.

This new world religious understanding is not merely some imaginary fiction or vague dream, but is something which is going to begin its process and evolvement now. And as soon as humanity is moving forward, a great **Revelation** is waiting to occur. The nature of this Revelation is not ready to be revealed as of yet, but humanity can live in expectation of this new Light that will be revealed. Humanity should embrace the spiritual teachings and be aware of the 'raining of knowledge' perpetually hovering over humanity. Remember, the 'rain' cannot distinguish need; it falls both on the ocean as well as in the valley.

One aspect which will occur in the future is the development of the oneness of humanity into a real and accepted fact. In the past much has been written and talked about this, but in reality, so little has been achieved. In fact, what has taken place is that the relationships between nation and nation, and people of different ethnic backgrounds have deteriorated and have gone from bad to worse. But humanity should not accept defeat in all the fighting and struggling taking place on the surface.

These conditions are certainly disturbing but every attempt should be made to help these storms cease through practicing and embracing universal love and universal compassion. Then you shall hear those quiet and insistent voices calling for your attention, and you will feel the vibrations of the new energies issuing forth from the spirit world and immersing into every sphere of human life. The immanent and transcendent power of God and Christ Consciousness will be invoked by spiritual people and groups throughout the world and will have pronounced results. These energies of love, tolerance and goodwill will be poured into the world of humanity.

The tide will turn. And the changes towards a better and happier world, The Great Tomorrow will emerge, and no power of evil will any longer prevent the coming of The Great Tomorrow. You will open your eyes and you will see this unfolding before you. You will open your ears to the beautiful tones of goodwill that will become the core of the relationships between humanity and nations, and will delete the harsh voices of hate from their positions of dominance.

Can you not envision the beauty of that which shall be manifested and be established, and which will step by step lead to improved human relationships and finally bring about the Kingdoms of God on Earth? All of this shall become a reality, and humanity will calm and silence the disharmony and voices of dissent and the selfish urges and tendencies by each person contributing their share of genuine goodwill.

These visions and promises of a new spiritually and an advanced future for humanity must inevitably be recognized. But nothing in life, even if predestined, can be acquired without it being deserved, and although the above will indeed become the future of humanity, humanity still has to earn all that it is to receive. Therefore, as to when The Great Tomorrow will be realized and brought into living practice lies into in the hands of humanity.

It is for humanity to exert itself to the outmost to achieve the ideals and goal that are within their souls, or otherwise nothing constructive will occur and life may even deteriorate until humanity wakes up again…and then there will be the effort made to move forward and upward with inspired new force to the goal that has been set. This applies to individuals, groups and races. In fact, all people are surrounded by these energies which are ready to carry humanity forward in the proper direction, and the only requirement is that humanity must open itself up and become receptive to these energies.

And how can this sensitivity and receptiveness be acquired? By humanity embracing universal love and universal compassion throughout the world. It is not important how the above is expressed, whether it may seem insignificant or whether it is something that might draw public attention.

The nature of these acts will, in fact, depend on many factors, and will be determined by each individual's abilities and capabilities as well as by the environment and public attention. What will matter, is the motive inspiring the action, and whether such acts are performed as a result of embracing universal love and universal compassion. Such acts must be offered as a gift, with joy in your hearts, for what you give, that is what you get in return.

There are people from all over the world and from many different religions that will recognize that all religions really emanate for the one great spiritual Source. They will become aware that all the hate and fighting over the ages between different factions of humanity, between nations, and worst of all, between different religions, were founded by limited vision and limited understanding, and based on such egotistical characteristics such as self-righteousness, the quest for power, envy and selfishness in many forms. They will come to the realization that we are all the children of God, brothers and sisters, and that God is our Father and Mother.

The Great Tomorrow is but an expression which is fundamentally the same age old truths, the same ancient wisdom, but with a different and new approach such as follows:

(1) **God is within each of us**: In the past the stress has been that God is somewhere referred to as heaven, which from His throne, somewhere in the outer spheres, has been ruling the destinies of humanity. In The Great Tomorrow it will be understood that every one of us, has the spirit of God within us.

(2) **That we are a spirit with a soul having a human experience:** In The Great Tomorrow emphasis and understanding will be on the eternal and immortal lives of our souls, that our souls evolve from one life time to another, from each life experience, on its path of ascension to becoming at one with God and Christ Consciousness.

Closely integrated with the evolving of our souls are also the laws of reincarnation and the Cause and Effect of our past lives' actions. In these teachings in this book I will be discussing these important principles, emphasizing the old but often times forgotten truth, that man shall reap what he has sown.

It is in the heart of every person, although perhaps not recognized, that we are being urged forward towards becoming at one with God and Christ Consciousness. During the early stages of this striving for spiritual evolving it may be by our instincts, but as The Great Tomorrow unfolds, the vision becomes clear and our efforts become more conscious and more purposeful.

It shall become understood by humanity that all men and women, all of God's children have the spirit of God inside of them. We are part of God, and God is part of us. That is the gift that God has given to us, and why we are immortal and our spirit and souls are eternal. And humanity shall come to understand that the experiences that we have as humans are to allow us to evolve, until we become at one with God and Christ Consciousness and reach spiritual perfection.

Humanity will indeed come to realize, as I have been teaching in my previous books and talks, that we are all brothers and sisters, and each of us are at our own particular stage of spiritual development, as explained in the example of my 1000 step pyramid within each of us.

It shall come to be accepted that life on earth can be, and should be a wonderful experience, with each person embracing universal love and universal compassion towards one another.... and displaying goodwill and love in our daily interactions with one another, as I shall explain and describe in my next chapter.

One of the greatest truths which humanity has not understood in the past is the divine relationship between every person, humanity as a whole and its Creator. In the current religious scriptures that have been offered are vague descriptions of God, as well as our having been given the impression of sinful people asking and praying to a stern God for the Lord's favors. But in reality, the truth is just the opposite.

There is only a God of love, who truly has a loving interest in his children who are experiencing the human experience. Once a deeper and more conscious understanding is developed between humanity and God, of which each individual is an integral part of God, it will then be realized by humanity that there exists a reciprocal attraction and approach, that of the Father/Mother towards his children, and that of the children towards their father/mother.

The realizing of these changes will take time, and it stands to reason that mistakes will be made, causing delays, but meanwhile humanity will have its feet on the Path towards this holy destination.

The journey has begun. Attainment of this ultimate goal can no longer be prevented by any adverse powers, but how quickly these ultimate goals are achieved will depend on the consecration and persistence with which humanity applies itself to these demanding but rewarding tasks. Now let us move on to our next chapter, The Vows, and as to how we attain these goals.

## Chapter Three

# The Vows

In 2011, following the publication of my book, *Time for Truth*, I decided to create a website that would allow people to post their own comments as well enable me to share with them the messages that I am given and my mission. The website became a huge success with people all over the world joining me, to form what we refer to as our spiritual family. Many thousands visit our site weekly now, some as only visitors and others to post their comments and responses to me and to each other.

Many wonderful miracles have happen on my website, www.nickbunick.com including it having channelled messages from Jeshua (Jesus), Mother Mary, from Oneness and a miraculous event that occurred in the sacred chapel built by Sara O'Meara, who is a living saint. Sara and I were praying together one day in the chapel when this miracle occurred and I taped what was told to us. It has been transcribed and is also shown on my website.

Some have asked if the entity that gave us this message was Jeshua (Jesus), or an angel or a spirit guide. We have instructed not to answer that question, but have been given permission to share that message word for word, which can be found on our site, www.nickbunick.com.

On our site we are committed to help one another evolve spiritually, to ascend our symbolic pyramid within us in order to become at one with God and Christ Consciousness.

Although I am not clairvoyant or clairaudient, I am claircognisant in that I am constantly given information from the spirit world, either through channelled messages that I write down or type as they are received or through some sort of telepathic means in which the information is transmitted to me mentally. I am also clairsentient, in that I feel the emotions of others.... One day I was instructed to begin a series of vows for my spiritual family members that would have an impact on their lives as well as the lives of those with whom they come in contact.

The very first vow deals with the need of people to meditate, and the tremendous difficulty so many people have, including myself, in actually being able to truly mediate as it is usually literally described.

I have talked to many highly advanced spiritual people, even some from India, who have acknowledged to me that they find it also difficult meditate, that it is a challenge to keep the mind still, no matter how many "ohms" they chant. The first vow given to me by the spirit world to share on my site, and now with you, my readers, is a form of meditation that is the most successful and peaceful one I have even been exposed to.

## VOW # ONE
## YOUR EDEN

Are you ready to start the lessons being given to me by spirit? My challenge is, there have been so many given to me, they are scrambled around in my soul mind, and I must unscramble them and put them in some sequence that will make sense....we shall refer to them as The Great Tomorrow vows, and today we shall deal with vow #1. "Every day I shall make an effort to become at one with that part of God inside of me."

People meditate to become at one with their higher self, that part of God inside of them. But the meditation they tell you to do is one which they say you must still your mind, which is difficult to accomplish.

As I have written earlier, I have discussed meditation with some of the most highly evolved spiritual people in the world, even some from India. They have acknowledged to me that meditation is a challenge, but we shall use a technique that spirit gave me for you (and me,) that is simple, gives us great pleasure and allows us to experience moments of serenity and love and joy as if we had temporarily reached step 950 of our pyramid.

Every one of us has a special place in our lives that gives us joy when we visit. We are going to go to this special place in our imagination, twice a day, once earlier in the day and once in the evening. And we will visit this special place, which we shall call your "Eden" and if you do not have one, you shall create one. It is your special place that brings you joy and serenity. To some, your Eden may find you walking through a forest. It is fall and the leaves have changed colors.

Under your feet you can feel crunch of the fallen leaves, and you can hear the sound of wild life and the birds in the background....to another, your Eden may find you lying on a blanket on a warm spring day. You are looking up at blue sky filled with white fluffy clouds, and you can hear the voices of your children or your grandchildren laughing in the background. And you are at peace with the universe.

You may select any surrounding that you choose, whether it be a garden, or in a forest. My Eden is walking along the shore of the ocean. I can feel the warm sand under my naked feet. I can hear the silent roar of the ocean, and the occasional call of a graceful sea gull. I can look across the horizon at this infinite body of water, and I know there is a man walking on the other side of the world, along this same ocean, looking across his horizon at me, and we are in sync with one another and the universe.

To go to your Eden, you must select a quiet place, where you are by yourself. It is your Eden, where for those ten minutes you will become at one with God and universal consciousness. Do not despair if you miss it one morning or one evening. It is okay. There is no guilt for it is your p be there, in serenity, in peace of mind and at one with God.

It may take you a week, or two weeks, but it is okay, for time does not exist in your Eden. ...but I say to you, you must commit to go to your Eden twice a day (although occasionally you won't be able to) but the effort must be there. And we ask that you share that experience with us on this site, once you find what it is like to be at one with divinity, in your Eden.

## VOW # TWO
## YOUR SOUL MIND

Are you ready for vow #2? ...In vow #1 we went to our Eden, the place we feel peace and harmony, a place to rejuvenate our souls, and if you did not have an Eden, you were encouraged to create one

Vow #2 is recognizing our soul mind and using it in our interactions with others at all times. What is our soul mind? What I am sharing you as a definition is not to be confused with what scientists or psychologists try to define, but from a spiritual perspective.

Our conscious mind is the mind we use to receive information, to interpret and respond with. It receives its instructions from either your ego or you soul mind. Your soul mind is that part of you that is the compliment to your spirit, your higher self and the spiritual world.

When you witness someone performing an outstanding achievement, your ego wants you to feel envy and jealousy, but your soul mind wants you to show admiration and appreciation.

When you see a person on the street that is in shambles and unkempt, your ego wants you to feel disdain, but your soul mind wants you to have compassion for that person.

When someone behaves in a manner that you feel is rude to you or lacking respect, your ego wants you to respond in anger, but your soul mind wants you have tolerance and respond with gentleness and love.

When you witness someone performing below par, your ego wants you to express criticism, but your soul mind want you to give encouragement.

When you see another that is in need of help, you ego mind wants you to ignore that person, but your soul mind wants to be generous and provide support.

When there are opportunities for you to benefit yourself from another by being deceitful or lying, your soul mind wants you to always be honest and truthful.

When you accomplish something you are proud of, your ego mind wants you to boast and brag, but your soul mind wants you to be humble and have humility (for your soul mind knows you will be greater appreciated by others complimenting you, rather than you complimenting yourself.)

When faced in uncomfortable situations, your ego mind wants you to feel fear, but your soul mind wants to have courage.

When someone provides you with help, your ego mind wants you to believe you are entitled to that help, but your soul mind wants you to express gratitude.

We are constantly being exposed daily to dozens and dozens of challenges and situations that we have to respond to. You control your mind, your mind controls your responses and your actions. It is your decision if you wish to live your life being ruled by your ego, or by your soul mind, that gift you were given by God which is the partner of your spirit, and that part of God inside of you.

Two evenings ago I was watching my son play basketball for his high school and we were out of town, at our opponent's gym. Our team was ahead by about 12 points and there were about 10 teenage boys to our left in the stands from the other school, that were loud and screaming and stomping their feet every time our boys were going to shoot.

The parents around me were getting very upset, as was I, and I was going to say something to them. But then I thought through my soul mind, and instead, I realized they were just kids enjoying themselves, and my soul mind kicked in and I sent them my love and tolerance.

You must be aware of these choices you will have many times a day. You are the one that makes the decision as to whether you show disrespect or respect, bigotry or acceptance. Pause before you react to a situation or to another person, and remind yourself that you want to react with your soul mind and not your ego.

Eventually your ego will realize it has been turned off and you can place it into a compartment and seal the door and not have to deal with it again for your soul mind and you will become at one with one another. It is a wonderful feeling you will have every time you know you have that choice, which mind to use, and you make the right decision. You are basically taking the love and compassion you felt for others while in your Eden, and now using it as you meet your daily challenges outside of your Eden. …Begin now, this moment, and experience the love and joy you feel inside as your soul mind helps you climb the stairs of your pyramid.

## VOW # THREE
### BE LOVE AND KINDNESS

Time for vow #3...but first, let's review vows 1 and 2. In Vow #1 had you created you own Eden, a place for you to visit to feel serenity, calmness, peace of mind and heart...a place to prepare you for the challenges of the rest of your day...Vow #2 was to make you aware of the differences between your soul mind and your ego mind; to "react" in your daily encounters and challenges with love and compassion, not in anger and insensitivity. In most cases it was to learn how to automatically react to situations in a positive way rather than in a negative manner.

With Vow #3, you learn to live your life with love and kindness and all around you, you shall create the same.....We come into contact with hundreds of people every day, some we know real well, such as our family, our friends, our co-workers...and we also come into contact with many dozens of people in a normal day that we barely know, who are strangers. We can make a difference in their lives which reflects also on our own lives, so we may evolve spiritually, ascending up the stairs of our pyramid.

With vow #3 we are going to make a 100% conscious commitment, that with every person we interact with, we will express love and kindness to them. I am referring to the waitress in the restaurant, the cashier in the store, the bundler who puts our groceries in the bags, the sales clerk in the shops, the strangers we walk by on the street as well as those we know well. We will give love and kindness to not only the ones that are already smiling, but to the grumpy people, the sad people, the ones that appear like they are struggling through their daily lives.

Love and kindness are contagious. If you smile at a stranger, almost always they will smile back. If you give to them love and kindness, that is almost always what you will get in return. But it is not what you get back that is important, it is what you are giving. You know that part of God is inside of you, and you are a walking living temple of God.

You are going to be in touch with that part of God inside of you by expressing to others the gifts that God has given to you as an enlightened spirit, that indeed you are, (or you would not be reading this book) …You will be amazed at the impact you will have on people all around you. They will feel your love and kindness and you will make a difference in their lives, even if it is only for a few moments.

To keep us reminded of the commitment of vow #3, I am asking that you keep count of how many people's lives you have impacted each day, including your family and loved ones and close friends. Keep an actual count in your head of every one of them, and write down on a piece of paper each night the number of lives you touched with vow #3.

In your postings, write, "I touched the lives of 18 people today," or whatever the number was. Some of you will have amazing stories to tell of the reactions that you created by "being love and kindness and creating the same all around you" ….Make that commitment, and vow #3 starts right now!

## *Vow # FOUR*
### *CONTROL YOUR THOUGHTS*

Vow#1 dealt with finding your Eden, to create a place of serenity and calmness. Vow #2 was to help you recognize that we should respond to meeting the challenges in our daily lives by using our soul mind rather than our ego. Vow #3 was designed to have us be love and kindness and all around us create the same.

Vow #4 deals with a challenge we all have, every day of our lives. It has to do with the thoughts we put into our minds, which then controls our emotions, our actions and our behaviour. We all realize that we should not eat contaminated food, for to put food that is contaminated into our body causes sickness and poor health. And yet, we are constantly putting contaminated thoughts into our mind, without realizing it or denying it access

What is a contaminated thought? It is one which translates into anger, hostility, jealousy, fear, embarrassment, or negative feelings. The subconscious mind cannot distinguish an event happening only once, as opposed to happening over and over again. If you have something happen to you that created embarrassment or fear, every time you think of that event, the subconscious mind thinks you are experiencing that event again, rather than it having happened just once. So you are hurting yourself letting yourself re-experience that negative thought.

Your mind plays a very major role in your health and happiness and the influence that you have in the happiness and joy of others. I have written in one of my books that if you plant an onion seed in the ground, it grows an onion. If you allow a negative thought into your mind, it creates negativity in you and in your temple of God, which you are.

You have to learn to control what goes into your mind. It is an area of importance that you will have your entire lives and those who do not control negative thoughts from being a constant part of your lives will experience poor mental and as well as physical health. That is why forgivingness is so important. Play a game with yourself. Every time a negative thought appears, call out silently "Red alert! Red alert"!

We shall call vow #4, controlling your mind, not allowing in negative thoughts.

## Vow # FIVE
### FORGIVENESS

Let us move into vow #5...but at the same time, always incorporating the first four vows into your daily life: 1) Your Eden.... a place to relax, find peace, find God; 2) using your soul mind rather than your ego mind when we have that choice; 3) being love and kindness and all around you creating the same; 4) releasing negative thoughts, not allowing contaminated memories and thoughts into our temple.........and now Vow #5, forgiveness.

Forgiveness accomplishes many things, but most importantly, it is for you, for it cleanses your soul. When you forgive somebody, they may not even appreciate it or care, but you have released toxics from your temple. You will no longer harbor feelings of hatred, anger, frustration, revenge and contempt of another. You have released that poison from your soul. It doesn't even make a difference if they accept your forgiveness, or are worthy of it. You have done your part in the eyes of God and Christ Consciousness.

If you could forgive every person and everything that has ever caused you to have those negative emotions, you would know the feeling of being a purer soul. You do not have to have a relationship with them. But you have truly opened the gates of your soul and said, "Out you guys, Misters Hate, and Anger etc. You are no longer welcome into my home, for my temple is now clean and filled with only emotions of love, kindness, compassion and joy".

The time to start is now. Get a pen and paper and write down the names of every person you have negative emotions about, and place their names on your "people to forgive" list. Rank them beginning with the ones you have negative feelings about the least, and start with them.

Years ago, one of my best friends in the world told me that of all the people he ever met in his life, he disliked me the least. What a compliment. He still is one of my closest friends today, although many miles apart. (He was the one in my book, *Time for Truth*, that was in the car with me going over the Sierra Mountains when the angels saved our lives.

When you contact people to tell them you forgive them, you can either do it in person, by phone or e-mail. You don't even have to tell them why. Some may cry and tell you they love you. Others may tell you they don't give a damn and start yelling at you, and that is the time for you to use your soul mind, and tell them that is okay. God gave them free will, but you forgive them any way.

No arguments, no confrontations, just forgivingness and pure love and kindness from you, and gratefulness for being able to cleanse your temple of God. As you get into the higher numbers, the ones that you really don't like, it may be more difficult, but you are now an experienced forgiver, so it really won't be that difficult and you will get even greater joy from forgiving them. Go for it. And we want you to share those experiences with us.

## *Vow # SIX*
### *CONTROL YOUR DESTINY*

Let us move into vow #6...but at the same time, always incorporating the first five vows into your daily life: 1) your Eden, a place to relax, find peace, find God, 2) using your soul mind rather than your ego mind when we have that choice 3) being love and kindness and all around you creating the same, 4) releasing negative thoughts, not allowing contaminated memories and thoughts into our temple.........and now 5) forgiveness.

So now let us move forward to vow #6. I have written in my book, *Time for Truth*, that we are all on different journeys to the same destination, that destination being to become at one with God and Christ Consciousness. But during the journey, which is called "your life", you can choose to be whomever you wish...for you are the script writer, the choreographer, the director, the producer and the star of that show, called "your life".

We can look back at different times of your past, and recognize there were times you wish you had written a different script. Perhaps you were too shy in high school or college, so did not have the friends or social life you wish you had.... or you wish you had been more light hearted and relaxed during school, so people did not take you as seriously as they did...or you were more aggressive in your job ten years ago, so you might have moved "up the ladder" faster. I can think back on my own life, and in any given period, and wish I had been different in some aspect of my personality or attitude that would have benefited me if I had. I am sure the same is true with every one of you...but we can't go back and change the past...but we can definitely do something about the present and future.

What aspect of yourself would you like to change? Do you wish you are more patient? Do you wish you are more fun loving? Do you wish you take life more seriously? Do you wish you are stronger in sticking up for the things you believe in?

Do you wish you wouldn't allow people to take advantage of you? Do you wish you are more demonstrative in showing love to the people you do love? We are the most complicated living thing on earth, and there is no other person like you. And everyone of us has areas in our lives we would like to improve upon if we had the opportunity….and now, you are being given that opportunity.

This requires great self-truth and self-analysis on your part, as well as being honest and objective with yourself. Write down on a sheet of paper how you wish to change. Do you want to be thinner, do you want to be more spiritual, do you want to have more patience, do you want to be more discerning, or fun loving or whatever?

It is your life. You create who you want to be, how you want to change. Only you have the ability and the right to do that, for this is your movie. Write that new script, and be a great producer and director so that you have the part down in expert fashion that you play, "this is my life".

Make those changes so dramatically and do it "*now*", so that others say to you, "What has changed about you"? Do it today. Do it now…and share it with us. Let us help you win an Oscar in your new role, in your play called "your life".

## Vow # SEVEN
### THE 3 C'S + 1

Vow #7. Are you ready for vow #7? Most of the vows you have received so far, except for creating and visiting your Eden, had to do with your relationship with other people in your lives. Vow #7 is one that is designed to help you learn to enrich your own life. Let's call it incorporating the 3 c's + 1 into your life. Those three c's + 1 are living your life with courage, confidence, commitment and passion . Easy to remember, these 3c's + 1. Let's look at each of them together as well as separately.

Passion- Life often is routine and to some people, boring. It does not have to be that way. Whether it be in a simple conversation with a friend or family member, going to the store, making a phone call…do every act and every function with passion. You are a child of God and you are one of a kind. There is no other person in the world like you. Live your life, every moment of it filled with passion and a zest for life. Whether by yourself or around others, fill yourself with passion and let it out, in every act you perform.

Courage- Have the courage to try things in your life that you haven't tried before…to speak your mind over things you were afraid to say…to show the world that you are special and have no fears. Throw the word embarrassment out of your vocabulary along with the word timidness. Be an example for others. Be a tiger, not a pussy cat. Use your courage to express your passion for life.

Confidence- Believe in yourself. Why wouldn't you? You are a person who lives your life with courage and passion. Do you have any idea how special you are? You know you are a child of God and that the spirit of God is within you, for you are part of God and God is part of you. How powerful is that? How can you not be filled with confidence, considering the courage and passion that emanates from your very soul?

Commitment- Make that commitment right now to incorporate the 3 c's +1 into your life, right this moment. Starting right this second. You make that commitment right now and then no one, no one, can take that away from you.

If I had any achievements in my life, it is because I committed myself to live my life with passion and courage and had the confidence in that commitment. See how they are all interconnected? And **you** can live your life that way also. These are not abstract words. They are a way of life and they are yours to incorporate and become a part of who you are. Go for it.

I encourage you to incorporate these seven vows into your life today, now. And read this chapter daily until you do, and then once a week, as a reminder. It will change your life forever, and also make a major impact on the lives of others that come in contact with you daily.

Let us explore in the next chapter the understanding of God and Life. What is the relationship between God and Life and are we capable of understanding these two concepts?

## Chapter Four

# God is Life

Our planet should be considered a living entity, the physical manifestation of God. It animates and personifies all that is found in our existence. It is in this one entity that we live and have our very being. It represents the essence of everything, the soul Life of the Earth with all that it contains.

It is impossible to conceive that a galaxy, a man or an atom ever having a separated or detached existence. Each and every form and particle is part of the One Life, and each form is part of existence. They are all part of One Life, and each form is but a minute fraction of a greater form, and every form in turn is again an aggregate of larger subsidiary forms of life. A quality which interrelates and binds each and every Form throughout the universe into the ONE WHOLE.

The interfacing and combining of the essence of life with substance produces consciousness that which is the reflecting of the soul. The degree of consciousness will vary according to how receptive is its form, with where is the point in evolution of the form, and with the relative position it occupies in the overall chain of development.

God is a concept beyond the limited understanding of the human mind, and because God is Life, it is consequently just as futile to attempt to explain what life is. There are those who are under the delusion that man may someday succeed in creating new life, but these ambitious individuals do not understand that Life can never be created, because all that exists already contains life.

Every form in existence, regardless of its simplicity or complexity is already a manifestation of life, whether it be mineral, vegetable or animal. Life is **that** power which sustains the form and which consistently demonstrates its presence by some kind of activity or 'livingness'.

Life is but another manifestation of energy, and as a divine principle it can never be destroyed. From a spiritual aspect, it is therefore impossible to "take life" for one can only pass on the essence of life from one form or channel it to another, from one life experience to the next, until eventually the Will of God is realized.

Life should never be taken indiscriminately and in this respect it follows the dictates of humanity's conscience or its intuition and laws, as well as humanity's soul's evolvement. What is unique about humanity is that each of us has the spirit of God within us, but we also have a soul, which has been given by God the gift of free will, the ability to establish values, to determine right from wrong, to evolve and ascend from one lifetime to another until each individual ascends to become at one with God and Christ Consciousness.

It is then that one can permanently relinquish the process of cyclical returns to the world of matter. It is then that the portals are opened for entry into the reality of LIFE where there will no longer be the need of a physical body insistently trying to sustain itself from living off of lesser forms.

In this regard it should be understood that **sacrifice** is one of the basic laws of our life system, and that through sacrifice the fundamental Plan and Purpose which sustains all existence is brought to fruition. And part of that plan is that the higher forms of life sustain themselves from the lower forms, with the lower life forms yielding itself to the greater, thereby incurring increased responsibility upon the greater.

The gift of free will is one of the most distinctive and important aspects of man in that consciousness and free will are so integrated with one another. Free will constitutes one of the most essential requirements for human evolvement, and it therefore is a factor that must never be overlooked or interfered with.

It is through free will that we make a conscious effort and commitment to live our lives embracing or not embracing universal love and universal compassion. It is through free will, that we either ascend closer to becoming at one with God and Christ

Consciousness or descend, separating ourselves further from our soul's purpose in Life and our soul's mission.

And so the Wheel of Life forever keeps revolving and evolving, in each form, mineral, plant, and man; evolving in humanity from the beginning, from basic animal instinct, and then through the emotional, to the mental, and into to the SOUL development; and still for ever on and on…from lesser light to greater light…until we become at one with God and Christ Consciousness and only then we will then be able to truly comprehend God and Life.

Let us next explore the concept and understanding of reincarnation.

## Chapter Five

# Reincarnation

For those who are spiritually advanced, the concept of reincarnation is not an abstract belief based on a theory. For those people it is a well established fact that has accepted and been known in Ancient Wisdom for thousands of years, and has been subsequently proved over and over again in daily life. The principle is primarily based on the duality of humanity, that we are both mortal as well as immortal.

Those who cannot or will not accept the fact than we are a duality with an immortal spirit and soul which, during incarnation, functioning in a material body with which it is intimately associated with, may not be ready for these studies. Your understanding may come either later during your present life, or otherwise may have to wait until you have a later incarnation. But as I have said many times in my other books, we are not humans who by coincidence have a spirit and soul; we are spirits with a soul that are having a human experience.

For those who are doubters, it may be of value to you to know that I did not believe in reincarnation until I was well into my adult years. It was then that I had the experience, as described in detail in my first book, *The Messengers*, of having been given the entire memory of a person that lived 2000 years ago that you know as the Apostle Paul. I will not go into the details of those memories or my experiences of two thousand years ago, for that is not the purpose of this book. But I do know there were many thousands that did not believe in reincarnation until they had read that book which became a New York Times Best Seller.

Once you have accepted the premise of the immortality of the human soul, then logic, when not obstructed by dogma, will compel you to the conclusion that reincarnation is inevitable. If the composition of humanity is considered, with its many races and nations, with its variety of skin colors, languages, physical, emotional and mental characteristics, then some idea of its complexity will be better appreciated.

The point that I am emphasizing is the disparity between these individuals. Among the billions there are those that die of starvation, and those who die from excess, those who possess nothing, and those who require many people to manage their personal possessions.

There are those who still live as slaves, in comparison to those who have the power to dispose over the welfare of others, and the life and death of millions; there are those who are imbeciles and those with gifted brilliant minds; there are those who are wasting their bodies and those who are radiant with good health. And similarly, one could name many more contrasting conditions and characteristics. But finally there are those who are interested only in their own well-being, in contrast with those advanced souls who are characterized by spiritual love, living their lives committed to serving humanity.

If a person was only granted one life on Earth, only a single opportunity to either succeed or fail, and with all these individuals so unequally equipped for life's challenges and struggles, how could such a state of affairs be justified and considered to be fair? How could one possibly believe in a God of love apparently favoring one with every conceivable advantage in life, and to another, nothing.....no intelligence, no worldly goods, no opportunities, and no spiritual consciousness?

How could two divergent lives be brought into the world is such diverse conditions and not be given the same opportunities to experience life, to ascend and evolve in their goal to become at one with God and Christ Consciousness? Impossible, for no loving creator would allow such anomalies to exist, in which we were to be provided just only one opportunity to ascend and evolve and to understand our relationship with God, our creator.

And what of the life and soul of a baby or young child who experiences death at a very early stage of their lives? If they only experienced one lifetime, they would never have been given the opportunity to have use of their free will, to distinguish between right and wrong, to have made moral judgments, to have had an opportunity to understand their relationship with God.

The Church has taught since the 4th century that these infants would go to some place called limbo. There must be hundreds of millions of babies stored in limbo. I have discussed those absurd false teachings in my book titled *Time for Truth*, and prefer not wasting your valuable time refuting that nonsense again in *The Great Tomorrow*.

Fortunately for humanity we do have a loving Creator, one whose wisdom and just humanity we can believe in. The shortcomings lie with humanity itself who can neither understand nor interpret that which we have been provided. Humanity has been able to distinguish only a small facet of the Truth of an extraordinary profound system and therefore formed its understanding on totally misleading information.

Where has humanity failed in its reasoning? The answer and crux of the whole problem lies in the false teachings that the evolution and redemption of the human soul must be completed in a single lifetime on Earth. As I explained In detail in my book, *Time for Truth*, this began in the 4th century when the Catholic Church distorted the teachings of Jeshua (Jesus) who himself had stated that John the Baptist was the reincarnation of the prophet Elijah who lived centuries earlier.

The Church wanted people to believe that salvation and redemption could only be achieved in one lifetime and only through the Church and that is why in 553 A.D. at the Fifth Ecumenical Counsel in Constantinople the Church declared that anybody that continued to preach reincarnation would be excommunicated from the Church and there would be a curse on them.

Yes, the many differences between individuals are factual and they do form part of the pattern of human existence, but once the reasons for these differences are understood, there should no longer remain any doubt about the compassion and love of our Divine Creator.

What we are observing in individuals are merely the current outer expressions in the stages of development attained by the many components of humanity, all of whom are in a state of constant change. Some are at a lower level of evolvement and spiritual ascension, and others being well advanced up the stairs of their pyramid, becoming closer to that part of God within them and Christ Consciousness.

Humanity would evolve so much faster if it understood the Truth. What would be understood is that our mortal life is only the physical instrument which is temporarily occupied by our God given immortal spirit and soul. Our material bodies will no longer exist at the end of its life span, but our souls, together with the true essence of our eternal lives are transferred to one of the etheric levels, depending on the spiritual development achieved in our current lifetime, that being, how high a person has climbed the steps of his or her pyramid.

Existence continues on these higher spiritual planes except that the soul will now be free and no longer encumbered by a limited physical mortal body. After our sojourn within this spiritual world, which in earth years could be a short or a long period, we will eventually develop an urge or need for further earthly experiences and to be born again.

Your spirit is part of God's spirit which gives you your immortality and your soul is a reflection of your spirit, its personality, its current values and attitudes, and the memory and product of all its lives' experiences. It must have these lifetime experiences in order to evolve, so your spirit is in a perpetual state of change and evolution with every experience that you have in the material world. Your soul continues to experience and evolve until it becomes at one with the essence of our Supreme Creator. What humanity must understand is that your soul needs these experiences, and that is why we do experience our human lifetimes.

Millions of years ago homo sapiens were chosen as the species on this planet that our souls would occupy to experience this soul growth. This species provided our souls the ability to have dexterity of hands and feet, and vocal cords to use to communicate with one another.

The only influences exerted on these original primitive bodies in the beginning was to provide them with the self-consciousness needed to distinguish themselves from the animal world. For innumerable incarnations covering millions of years these reincarnations were repeated, the soul gradually developing from bodies and needs focused exclusively on satisfying the physical aspects of existence and survival.

Eventually our souls gradually evolved towards emotional life experiences and the development of our mental faculties. Once our souls started on that pathway, many different doors were opened for new experiences and development.

The above information may help you understand the wide diversity in type, quality, characteristics and development that occurred among the billions of individuals which today mankind comprises. Every person's journey from the beginning of your soul's first lifetime has happened over millions of years and every journey has been unique and one of its kind. So there is no question of an unjust Creator favoring one person, or race, or community or nation over another, rewarding some and penalizing others, for what we are observing are merely stages of expressions of a soul's journey, like reading one page of a book that consists of five million pages.

To humanity's judicious eye some of these experiences may seem unnecessarily harsh or cruel, but to our limited human understanding, it may be exactly what that soul needed to experience at that specific stage. We are today observing the human panorama of several billions of individuals each guided by its own indwelling soul, each at its own particular stage of evolutionary development. Each soul is in the process of gathering additional experiences on its long, long journey back to its original home, that of our Creator, becoming completely at one with God again.

Remember, even if a person is at a very low step of their pyramid, we are still all on the same path. Every soul has endured and will be enduring the same experiences in past, present and future lifetimes, and eventually will arrive at the same destination, only to proceed ever again, still further, on the eternal evolutionary path to the mysterious unknown.

Regarding the time period in between incarnations, do not place too much emphasis on this issue, as wide differences occur in comparing the time periods that these occur. Some souls linger for very, very long periods in earth years between incarnations before deciding to return to the mortal world while others return very rapidly.

Generally speaking, those that experienced very little evolving in their last lifetimes reincarnate much sooner. Such was the case of my last lifetime which I described in my book, *Time for Truth*, where I had died at the age of twenty-two after graduating from the Sorbonne Universality in Paris and was drafted into the French army and killed in Belgium in the First World War.

As your spiritual development proceeds, usually there is a longer time between incarnations, so that much more time is spent in the spiritual world than in the mortal world, judged in earth years. However, as more and more advanced spiritual people are needed in humanity, their returns to Earth will happen faster for they are needed as spiritual leaders for humanity.

Normally the decision to reincarnate is made by the soul itself. When this happens, your soul, assisted by a group of specialized spiritual helpers will select suitable parents for your new incarnation. These parents are selected with care, with due consideration given to the environment which they will provide you. Your soul is returning for specific purposes, so it is important that the selection of your parents and that environment is suited to provide you the experiences that your soul needs.

It could be an environment of hardship, of challenges and struggles; or it could be an environment of many opportunities, special gifts and doors ready to be opened for you. It is directly related to your karma and the experience that you need to be exposed to on your own soul's journey. It is not to punish you or reward you, but to help you along your journey to become at one with God and Christ Consciousness.

I will also share with you that souls often return in groups, so that they will experience their new lifetime with other members of that group. The degree that these group members will be associated with one another during this new lifetime will vary greatly. Some may be born into the same families, some may meet early in life and others very late in life.

It will vary greatly and your soul mind and their soul mind will recognize each other through your soul minds and transfer the emotions and feelings to your conscious minds. You will feel a connection with that person, such as perhaps overwhelming love, and not consciously know why. Or you may feel animosity and hostility towards that person and also not know why.

Of course, it will be based on your past life experiences together. One person may have been your loving child or spouse in your last lifetime, or conversely so, your tormenter or torturer, whom may have made your life miserable.

Group bonds can play a very important role if they a based on a common bond to impact humanity, and the evolution of humanity. The members of a group can start revolutions, overthrow governments, create new societies, bring freedom and justice to their parts of the world, and change history forever, either in a positive or a negative way.

It is happening even today, as we look at events around the world. I do not have to point them out to you. Just look at yesterday's newspaper events, locally, nationally or worldwide, and you will see them enfolding before your very eyes.

As far as soul life in concerned your gender is irrelevant, since this is essentially an attribute of physical and emotional choice. For the sake of rounding off human experiences, the soul will however periodically choose to be born changing genders after many, many years of having the same gender. This will also provide you an understanding of the challenges to gays and lesbians. For example, a soul that has experienced many continuous lifetimes as a female now decides to experience being born as a female.

But that soul, in its first new gender incarnation will still have many of the attributes physically and emotionally as a female, as well as their female needs and desires. This may take several lifetimes to make the full gender transition, each additional lifetime as a male exhibiting fewer and fewer of the characteristics of femininity that were developed over many, many lifetimes as a female.

Of course, just the opposite is experienced when a soul that has lived most lifetimes as a male decides to make the gender transition as a female.

Very advanced souls who have been delegated some specific function in the service of humanity may be asked to delay their next incarnation or to expedite it. This will depend on the timing of world affairs, as to when they are most needed. This accounts for when the soul of Jeshua (Jesus) will return to Earth in human form again, as well as other past spiritual and world leaders in history. I am well aware as to how this applies to me as explained in detail in the New York Times bestselling book about me, *The Messengers*.

The contents in this book, *The Great Tomorrow* began to be brought to me several years ago, but I was not prepared to receive it then, understand it totally nor was I then capable of transcribing it into words that would have been understood by most people. It came from several different sources and was often so profound and complex and too difficult for me to process into the appropriate words.

Then something happened to me that changed that dramatically, so I can now share these words with you, which my spirit guides often refer to as The Truth, The Teachings or The Wisdom. I hope that you are benefitting from what we are experiencing together, for writing this material is having a profound experience on me also. In the next chapter we will explore and do a review of humanity's thoughts and actions in the past that have influenced the world we live in today.

## Chapter Six

# Review Over the Ages

Many scientists for many years have estimated erroneously that our planet was a few million years of age. It is now realized that our planet is many times older than that, and that the span of time covered by our present civilization is minute, to say the least.

Even just turning back the clock just 2000 years, when Jeshua walked the earth, we now know much of the information in the gospels is inaccurate and distorted, as I have described in my books *The Commitment* and *Time for Truth.* And if we were to go back into historical times as long ago as 3000 years before Jeshua's birth, we know practically nothing of what really existed, except for an occasional fossil or cave drawing.

This can be compared to pointing a flashlight into the darkness and although you can see what is the foreground of the small beam of the flashlight, you have no idea what is beyond that small beam of light, a world that continues on for thousands of more miles.

If humanity were to remain solely dependent on its own knowledge and scientific ingenuity, ancient and prehistoric facts will remain hidden forever. But for humanity to fully understand how it fits into the greater Plan, humanity should acquire an understanding of its origin and gradual evolution. Some of the arcane history is vaguely referred to in the Old Testament, but is so shrouded in parable and fairy tales, they are of truly no value.

Some will reject what I am going to share with you because it cannot be substantiated by factual data that can be confirmed. That is their choice as well as yours. I am not the source of the information that I will be sharing with you. I am but the conduit, the receiver of the information being provided from the spiritual world to you, and through your gift of free will, you may accept it or reject it.

To follow this journey with me, do not think in terms of years, or centuries, but in time frames of millions of years. Yes, we are going back 21 million years ago, when the animal that was to become a human walked around on his and her two feet, had no vocabulary or capability of judging right from wrong, and had no values and no free will. Yes, we are going back to the time when **we** were just another animal. This animal, this future species that was to become a human existed in that capacity that we are now going to envision for about four million years.

Then about 17 million years ago, the first signs of spirit and soul entered only into this specific species. They first began to gather as a group with an understanding that there was something different about themselves than the other animals in the central regions of South America where they lived.

Another grouping took place in Asia, and even today there are certain ancient monuments of these early primitive beings hidden deeply under the sands of the Gobi Desert. And then two million years later, approximately 15 million years ago, they finally evolved to be recognized as more human in behavior than as animals, and they settled in the area now occupied by the Pacific Ocean. They had mastered over these large time frames the ability to use words and communicate. They called their region Lemuria.

Another approximate three million years elapsed, and with it came their further development of their capacity to think and live. The greater part of their kingdom of Lemuria was destroyed by volcanic action and now lies under the sea, leaving only a number of small islands where once they had been a vast continent.

Many of the Lemurians survived and moved eastward, and they become the founders of that world we talk and write of, known as Atlantis, which stretched far out towards Europe and North Africa and is located where we now find the Atlantic Ocean. Very little knowledge is known of these two civilizations, but I shall provide you a general description of the various stages they evolved through.

The important event was the evolving of the souls that uplifted the Lemurians from living like animals to enter into the human kingdom, although barely noticeable for a very long time. Over time the gradual wakening of the self produced humans still largely retaining their animal tendencies, but beginning to distinguish themselves by their self oriented nature and a strong desire for satisfying their physical appetites.

On the emotional level, only basic feelings mainly still existed within them, such as fear of pain and sexual desires. At times there were beginning indications of the love nature, combined with an urge towards wanting something better, something of greater value, that in ages to come would develop into a form of aspiration. Please remember, we are still discussing a time in history 12 million years ago.

Of course it is impossible for us to clearly understand the mind, or rather , the lack of mind, of these ancient people whose level of existence totally differed from that of the present. But even today people at different levels of development find it extremely difficult to understand each other's mentality and approach to life, each group holding onto and accentuating those values which to them, in their particular stage of evolvement, appear to be so different than those of others.

The awakening of these principles of desire and emotion in these people prepared humanity for the Atlantean phase, where humans no longer remained satisfied with an unsophisticated type existence. The leaders of the Atlanteans began to display substantial firsts signs of mental progress, just as today within our Aryan society there are ever increasing signs of intuitional development.

The Atlantean mental growth was applied to wanting more material possessions for satisfying their ever increasing desires. The gathering of possessions inevitably led to the renouncing of certain freedoms which were being found in the nomadic lives of the hunters, and this in turn led to the establishment of larger and more permanent groups than just the family unit, eventually giving rise to the development of the first urban type communities.

In those early days of Lemuria and Atlantis the masses were led by their priests and kings, assisted by their supporters. With the development of the Atlantean race mainly focused on the stimulation of their desires, the era became characterized by an overruling tendency for excessive sexual relationships, resulting in a rapidly increasing population with low moral standards. In the course of time the damaging need of satisfying emotional desires lead to perversion and decadence. As happened previously with Lemuria, the destruction of Atlantis was the result of cataclysmic convulsions of the Earth's crust, and the eventual submerging of the greater part of Atlantis into the ocean, known as the Atlantic.

These events took place several millions of years ago, and the Atlantean civilization, including their buildings and structures still exist today lying under millions of years of accumulated debris under the ocean floor. A few large islands were formed and did survive the disaster, and these provided a sanctuary for the survivors. They then became the nucleus of the partial restoration and regeneration of our race and enabled humanity's evolutionary process to continue.

Then about 850,000 years ago the larger part of these islands were in turn swallowed by the sea, leaving only one relatively small portion west of the Pillars of Gibraltar, which Plato referred to in his writings as Poseidonis, or Atlantis. This remaining portion of land also disappeared below the ocean but not before a large number of the surviving population had escaped  and introduced civilization where they resettled, in parts of what we today know as Europe, the Mediterranean regions and the near and middle East.

It was this submergence of Antlantis that gave rise to the biblical myth of Noah's Ark.  Many of the stories in the Old Testament are based on experiences of the Atlantean survivors and their descendants. It was through their development did the perpetual conflict between good and evil and humanity's free will to choose between those alternatives emerge.

Throughout history our spiritual guides have tried to motivate, inspire and direct humanity's efforts. The teachings being provided in the past and in this book should enable mankind to successfully evolve to being at one with God and Christ Consciousnesses in spite of those who live in indolence, selfishness, perversity and misapplication of free will. The efforts of The Great Tomorrow's spiritual leaders and their Teachings will contribute to the Divine Plan and Purpose, and there will be a Great Tomorrow.

This history of humanity could also be seen as the history of humanity's approach to God, in our Creator always offering Light and contact with the Most Divine, and of the pouring out of that Light, like a beacon in the dark throughout our planet and our universe. It remains forever and is an irreversible Law that for every appeal issuing from the hearts of humanity, it must bring forth a commensurate response. And when humanity in desperation sounds forth a unified appeal, a World Teacher, a Spiritual Leader, shall always be brought forth by the Divine to bring new revelations, hope and leadership towards spiritual evolvement.

Humanity could, in a sense, be regarded as the cumulative effect of streams of divine energy from the spiritual world without interruption, being emitted onto humanity in its many varying stages of evolutionary development. All that has happened in the past and is occurring now in the present is the accumulative effect of these energies pouring systematically and cyclically through nature and through that part of nature called humanity.

It is therefore all related to the receiving and distribution, the sensitivity and reactivity of these divine energies, and of its absorption and dispersion among humanity. It is the embracing and application by humanity of universal love and universal compassion among all the people of the world that will enable this to become a reality. In the next chapter let us explore mankind itself, and what is the essence of human beings.

## Chapter Seven

# The Essence of Mankind

Within every living human is part of God's spirit which is a fragment of that which we know of as God, even though we must acknowledge that we truly do not have a comprehension with that in reality means. The most honest and informed scientists and doctors must admit that they cannot truly explain that which gives our bodies life. The physical body only represents the material refection of that which exists on planes outside of our world, a reality which humanity remains blissfully unconscious of.

A man or woman is the sum total of an intricate range of complexes, psychoses, neurosis, instincts, intuitions, physical skills, ambitions, and intellectual faculties which are the sum product created from numerous energies and forces from many sources. Some are environmental, some from past life experiences and some from spiritual influences that we are not even aware of.

An individual is limited to understanding and expressing no more than the condition of his or her nervous system and brain will permit. The degree to which one can do so varies depending on the development of that person between wide limits, ranging from the early Lemurian consciousness to that of the other extreme of divine perfection. Humanity represents a complete range of individuals encompassing all phases of development between these two extremes.

An individual is the product of a duality, that being matter and spirit. And the result of this union is that an individual is in reality a 'child of God', a singular divine unit whose essence is part of God. But this is rarely demonstrated by humanity in daily life. Yes, you are in reality spirit, manifesting yourself through the matter of your physical body. As I have written and spoken many times, and sometimes hear other individuals who represent themselves as spiritual leaders who adopt my words, "We are not human beings that by coincidence have a spirit and a soul, but we are spirits with a soul having a human experience".

The individual lives his or her life influenced by whatever forces or energies controls that person, and that person's behavior will depend on which has the greatest influence on that person, whether it be emotional, intellectual, their ego or their soul mind which predominates them. This is why I have placed such an importance on your practicing and using the vows in your daily lives, the vows that I shared with you in an earlier chapter.

An individual is therefore the aggregate of forces which dominate that person's life, that establishes his or her values, personality, beliefs and appearance. For ages humanity has been wielded and dominated by these forces, humanity's evolution being shaped accordingly.

As humanity progressively arrives at a clearer understanding of these forces and how they affect each individual, we will collectively and individually begin to discriminate between them and decide which are these we wish to most live our lives by and influence our behavior. It is God's intent that eventually the stage will be reached when your soul mind and your spirit will dominate, and that again is why I have placed so much emphasis on the vows I have shared with you.

The basic understanding that we are all the children of God, and therefore brothers and sisters could lead to the adage that all people are equal. This is correct to the point God has made each of us potentially equal, for we all are spiritual brothers and sisters and from one part of the one humanity. We all function within physical bodies that have been endowed with the spirit of God within us. We are all from the same origin and work towards the same final spiritual destination, to climb the steps of our pyramid until we are at one with God and Christ Consciousness. Therefore, as far as these divine attributes are concerned, we are all definitely equal.

As with all else in life, this basic assumption is however, of a relative nature, and can be very easily misconstrued. For example, in politics it is demanded that the practice be 'one man-one vote' without there ever being consideration to the fact that allowances are never made for the differences in the spiritual, mental and emotional development of the different individual voters.

An honest study of a typical community would show that only a relatively small percentage of the population is capable of independent and truly objective thought, and that the large majority have not outgrown the Atlantean stage. They are therefore able to be swayed or led to vote by effective emotional propaganda rather than what is a true understanding of what is in the best interest of the community, state or country. Therefore political systems based on slogans may accomplish their winning elections, but at the same time have very harmful consequences to the community, state or country.

Allow me to share another illustrative example. Visualize a school which has classes beginning for those in the first grade all the way through to students who are seniors in college. Even though all of the students of every grade are equal from a divine perspective, certainly no one would argue nor disagree that the students in the first grade do not have the knowledge or educational growth as those who are studying as seniors in their last year of college classes.

So every human being is the personification of a part of God's spirit, being impelled into an incarnation by the need for a human physical experience. All of God's children are striving towards the same final goal, but each individual must follow his or her own particular path to reach that destination, of evolving to become at one with that part of God within them and with Christ Consciousness. For lifetime after lifetime we return into physical incarnations to gain further experiences in the world of matter and to continue on its prolonged and difficult path, trying to climb those stairs of our pyramid to higher levels of ascension.

Every incarnation is undertaken with the purpose of supplementing past life experiences and to enrich and expand our souls by further tests and trials, to encourage the development of attributes that lead to higher levels of spiritual ascension. And that is why exactly alike identical individuals will never be encountered, for each of us is on a different stair of our pyramid, each individual influenced by its particular purpose in its current lifetime, by his or her character, attributes and capacities, which will be consistent with what step they have attained on their pyramid of a thousand steps.

You may ask, is it not possible for thousands to be on the same step, perhaps that being step 444. And I shall answer to you, that between steps 444 and 445, there are a thousand mini steps.

Those personal variations in quality and character will also be influenced by the surroundings and circumstances in which destiny has decreed so that particular individual could pursue his or her goals. This would be demonstrated by differences in race, color of skin, language, culture, and mental and physical characteristics...those qualities provided by divinity to compose that intricate tapestry of human living which in its totality resents the Divine Plan, not only for human development, but for the whole of Creation.

To have a greater understanding of how the soul finds expression during a human lifespan, it is important to know how humans are constituted, that they are differentiated from three aspects of elements, and how these elements co-ordinate together to form a single and effective operating unit, a person.

This individual, the personality, is composed of the physical, emotional and mental bodies, and they determine the person's temperament, profession chosen, and the quality of that person's daily activities. They will determine the person's reaction to impacting energies; they will provide the coloring of that person's character, abilities and aptitudes, deficiencies and limitations, which will collectively determine and influence that person's path through life.

These three influences will be discussed and analyzed for you in detail in the following chapter. Some of these concepts will be new to you, strange and perhaps difficult for you to accept, but as I go deeper into them, you will understand the beauty and logic of these teachings and they will be better appreciated. It will become apparent to you how perfectly these patterns begin to fit together to produce a picture of which, so far, only a vague outline has been revealed to you in this book, the essence of who you really are.

Have I gone too far? Have I lost you with too much information, some that in some ways was so simple, you thought, as you read, I always knew that; and other teachings that you think, I never considered that before? Many of you have traveled and journeyed with me through my other books, and on my website, so to you, some of these teachings sound familiar, and yet, there are many times you think, Nick never shared that with us before.

I have always told you that we are on a journey together. Now we are visiting places together that I haven't taken you before. But I know you are up to it, for otherwise 'Spirit' would not be telling me to share it with you. So fasten your seatbelts. You are going to be in for quite a ride and not just my usual spiritual family members on my website, www.nickbunick.com... but all of you. .....

## Chapter Eight

# The Constitution of Humanity

The manifestation in physical matter of the spirit of God with a soul, is a human being, you. It is so important for you to understand these words. The spirit of God united with a soul on this earth level, it is you, and every other one of God's children. The final objective of you and every individual is that your physical life and activities should eventfully be brought under complete and conscious control of your soul, at one with God and Christ Consciousness. In order to accomplish this goal, this process has to work through and with the energies of three types of forms which are:

The *mental body* which is the first aspect.

The *astral or emotional body* which is the second aspect.

The *physical body* which is the third aspect.

The mental body of an individual operates through that individual's free will, and seeks to co-ordinate the functions of his or her physical body, and is some respects endeavors to link up the consciousness of all the three forms, but it may also do the reverse and cause separation between them. ...The astral aspect deals with the quality of the individual, contains the psychic elements.... and the physical aspect is where consciousness or Spirit is reflected in the material form and in your physical being. The force holding together the three forms described above and allowing them to function as a coherent whole, is contained within the individual's *etheric body* which is controlled by your seven centers of energy, your chakras. These centers are responsive for the vitalization and co-ordination of an individual's body, and they co-ordinate these forms with the soul, the main center of consciousness. ..I did not tell you this part of the journey would be easy, and that is why I recommended that you put on your seat belt as we continued. Allow me to share some definitions with you that may be helpful.

The personality of an individual is the showcase of this triple concept. It is composed of the physical body which contains the dual aspects, both of the etheric body and the physical body and it also manifests the emotional or astral body as well as the mental body, including your mind. In other words, all three of these types of energies are manifested through your personality.

Your soul is the personality of your spirit, its values, that part of Christ Consciousness within you. Your soul is the link between the spiritual world and the physical world, the link between God and your physical body while you are living as a mortal. Your soul is what provides you consciousness, character and quality to all that exists in your life, and it is therefore the inner guide of your personality.

The level of spiritual evolvement that you are experiencing is directly related to how much influence your soul has on your life, until eventually you are fully controlled by your soul, and then the doors are opened for you to the highest spiritual influences in the spiritual world. Do you not see that this connection being described is consistent with the climbing the steps of the pyramid we have been discussing as well as the use of our vows? We are now examining these teachings from a higher perspective.

This Spiritual Triad is called the Monad and is the reflection of how our Creator functions at the mortal level, in that it is expressed as 1) spiritual will, 2) intuition, love-wisdom, Christ Consciousness and 3) the higher or abstract mind. The Triad has basically the same relationship to the Spirit of God, the Monad, as the Soul has to God's spirit that is within us, in which our soul is functioning through the Triad, which is at the higher level with God, the Monad. The Monad is Pure Spirit, which is God, reflecting the triplicity of Deity, which is 1) Divine will of the Creator, 2) The love and Wisdom of Christ Consciousness and 3) The Holy Divine Spirit, which you have witnessed if you have watched any of my healing shows on my website, in which I feel encompassed in that divine energy when I am praying for a healing and can feel it passing through me.  I know that those of you that have watched my healing show on my website understand what I am referring to, for you have witnessed it.

Some of you, as an individual, may be able to  relate to  what I have been sharing with  you these last several pages, because as a human,  your  spiritual  evolution  is  centered  around  your consciousness  and  its  gradual  development  as  you  progress, ascending the stairs of your pyramid.  It is when you reach closer to the top of your pyramid, to step 1000, that you become at one with God and Christ Consciousness and have the true awareness of what I have been discussing these last several pages.

But to reach the top, your journey of evolvement will be  through many lifetimes so   you may acquire the experiences that are necessary in the mortal world. You will live many diverse lifetimes, having many different characteristics;  skin colors varying between black, red, brown, yellow and white; you will experience lifetimes in bodies both as  male and female; live in the orient, the polar regions and in the tropics; you will experience want, famine, and abundance; the life of the slave and of the master.

Regardless of the experience you are having in any of the lifetimes mentioned above,   you are continuing to evolve and ascend nearer to the top, for none of those lifetimes are a deterrent to your goal, but are lifetimes that you chose before each incarnation is to help serve you to accomplish your goal. It is so IMPORTANT that you understand what I am sharing with you, for it also includes the lifetime you are presently experiencing right now.

My having described to you the Constitution of Humanity, which is the title of this chapter, may seem out of place to you. But I have done this deliberately, to confuse you. No, I am joking. I did it to provide you a background for visualizing and understanding the purpose and function as to why your spirit and soul has a physical body, as you do now, in your experiences of so many various lifetimes. I wanted to share with you the many influences that your mortal life has upon it, through its relationship with the Monad, the Spiritual Triad, which in essence, is God's soul.

Are you ready to move on, now that I have totally confused you…..  Where is it written that I do not have the right to have a sense of humor? The members of my spiritual family that know me from my previous books and my website are smiling right now, for they know me well.

Let's talk about the etheric body which literally encloses and interfaces with your physical body. Every atom in your body is surrounded by an electric energy field, which science refers to as the electro-magnetic field. Every form, whether it is minute, a person, or a planet, is composed of atoms, and these combined atoms individually retain their etheric substance which serves as the binding medium between atoms.

Throughout every physical form that exists, at the atomic level, there is a network of etheric matter which internally forms a dense grid, and on the outer surfaces intimately links and connects the form of the etheric body surrounding each and every form. The etheric bodies of all individual forms on our planet are again linked to compose the etheric body of the planet, as is the stars, or any heavenly body. Similarly all celestial bodies are synthesized by the cosmic ether into the One Universe, THE ONE DIVINE ENERGY, that we call God.

The cosmic etheric system is intimately connected with the tiniest atom and could be regarded as the nervous system of the Universe, through which all energies and forces are interrelated. It is the medium through which ALL FORMS are interrelated.

This network serves a double purpose.... as a medium for conducting the incoming and, simultaneously as an avenue for the outgoing forces. In the case of human beings it is along these etheric channels that contact is made to Higher Spheres and along these same paths responses are received and manifested.

In other words, in layman terms, this is how channeling is received by humans from spirit guides from the spirit world which can either be by the person writing down what is being channeled or through claircognisance, which is information going directly into the person's mind. I have experienced both of these methods of receiving information from the spirit world for many, many years, and much of this book is being written from information being provided to me from the spirit world.

This is not too dissimilar to mental telepathy found in our mortal world, or energy being transferred. Many photographs now exist of etheric effects upon plants and molecules when exposed to certain types of music, where there are significant changes in their atomic arrangement when classical music is played as compared to heavy metallic rock music.

Their atomic formations will vary between forms of beauty to ones of total disarray, depending on the music being played. This basically provides proof that plants not only show a form of consciousness, but definitely demonstrate an etheric reaction or a sense of emotion to events occurring around them.

Comparatively speaking, can you fathom the impact, comparing ourselves with human sensitivity versus that of plant life, that is made upon us as humans when we get exposed to different components in our environment? Whether this is true that it be different types of sounds such as found in music, or smells, whether they be rank smells or like a lilac; and visual experiences, such as watching a beautiful sunset or ocean and mountain scene versus viewing violence on TV or at a movie. No, the impact is currently beyond human understanding, or otherwise the world that our humanity created would be quite different.

The etheric body is a material body, although composed of much subtler material than the dense physical body. It is essentially a transmitter of energies, and not a generator of energies. It is a clearing house for all the forces reaching the physical body, and the conditions of your etheric centers will largely determine the extent which the flow of these forces are affected. Your etheric body is the receiver of your **Life Forces**, transmitting them to your physical body through your nervous system, your blood stream and your endocrine system.

The etheric body is the foundation and framework on which your material body is constructed, underlying and sustaining every part of your physical body. Any disability or congestion occurring in your etheric system itself, or any deficiency in the relationship or co-ordination between your etheric body and your physical body will immediately be reflected in your physical, emotional or mental condition. Free and unimpeded flows of energy between your etheric and physical body must be regarded as essential for retaining good health conditions.

The etheric body has no distinctive life of its own. With the "death' of your physical body, the etheric body is released from your body. I am not referring to your spirit and soul. I and my spirit guide have been teaching you about the etheric body being the material around you that allows the two worlds to meet, that being the spiritual world and the material world (mortal world).

The etheric body represents the most important feature affecting your physical body not only affecting your five senses and allowing you to function in the material world, but simultaneously providing you the channel for expanding the consciousness of your spiritual self as you evolve and ascend the stairs of your pyramid. (You might want to read this last section again, so it is fully understood.)

Your mortal body is composed entirely of numerous conduits of energy. At certain locations these lines cross each other and form points of centers of energy. Where many of these lines of energy cross each other, large centers of energy are formed, which create seven major centers which play a very important role in the functioning of your life.

These centers are situated in that part of your body which parallels your spine and surrounds your head. You may of heard people refer to them as your chakras. In addition to the seven major centers, there are twenty-one lesser centers and numerous transmitters of these energy nodes are distributed throughout your body. Although the seven major centers are usually referred to as being situated in your solar plexus, your heart, throat or head, this may be confusing as they do not actually occur within your physical body itself, but are distinctive focal points within your etheric body, situated in positions more or less corresponding to the organs they are associated with.

The seven major centers are the head center, the alta major center (spinal column), eye center (eyes, ears and nose), throat center (thyroid, vocal, lungs), heart center, solar plexus center (pancreas, stomach, sacral center (gonads, reproductive system), and the center at the base of the spine (spinal column, adrenal glands).

These seven centers are present in your etheric body in alignment to your physical body. During the life of the average person, some of these centers may remain more or less dormant, and when you are experiencing spiritual evolving, they will become active and energized.

I must caution you, if you try to use improper methods to fire up these energy centers through improper practices and by experimenting, it could cause you to damage your actual body or brain tissue, which could affect your health. So beware of people, even though their intentions may be good, that claim they can energize your chakra, for only you can do so, by evolving your spirituality.

To evolve spiritually you should live your lives as described in my chapter on vows and by embracing universal love and universal compassion. This would surely lead to accomplishing having your chakras energized and developed. In doing so, you are allowing your chakras to develop naturally rather than through artificial means, such as through listening to tapes, music, using crystals and other artificial methods

During this process of developing and energizing your chakras, you will find your centers of energy at various stages of unfoldment, some being dormant and others becoming very active. For most people the centers below the diaphragm will be more energized earlier than those above.

In other words, as you evolve spiritually, the heart and throat centers will develop at a slower rate than those chakras below them. As you continue to evolve spiritually, your head chakra, which involves your brain chakra, will become energized also, and then all your energy centers will become harmonized and coordinated together....You will know it when it happens, for I am experiencing it now, which is how I am enabled to write this book.

These energy centers, which I have been also referring to as your chakras, are distributors of energy to you, as if they were generators producing energy to your mortal body at different locations. And they are receiving their source from the etheric and astral world, so to speak, from our creator's energy. Are you getting all this, because tomorrow I am gong to give you a quiz....... Only kidding!

Continuing on, your physical body is functioning influenced by these centers of energy and combined into your whole being. Your *consciousness thread* is located in your head chakra and your *life thread* in your heart chakra. Each of your seven energy centers are related to different types of incoming energy being transmitted to you.

When the energy of your etheric body is not related to a particular chakra, then that charka remains dormant. An analogy might be having seven phone lines in your home, each with their own incoming number, and two are ringing and active, and five are not. So then when the phone is connected and rings on those two...... then they can receive the communication. So it is, when your chakra receives the energy it is related (connected to), it becomes vibrant, develops, and has a positive influence in your life.

All people differ from each other regarding the condition of their energy centers, just as we are different as to what step we are on our pyramids. That is, we all have different health situations, none being the exact same as another.

Some day this will be understood by the medical world, the physicians as well as the psychologists, and the medical scientists in the future will become knowledgeable regarding what I am sharing with you. This will aid them greatly in their being able to diagnose sicknesses, both physical and mental illnesses, and this understanding will aid them greatly in finding cures.

At some future time, when more is known and understood by humanity about our etheric bodies and our energy centers, highly spiritually evolved people will learn that they are able to control these chakras by their own power of thought. Then the energy centers will come under the control of you soul minds, which is something quite different than your conscious mind, as you now know. But is humanity ready for this yet?

With the exception of health conditions caused by accidents, wounds, infections or epidemics, most diseases are the result of disturbed conditions in one or more of your energy centers. This could mean one of your energy centers could be underactive or, conversely so, overactive.

A perfect example would be, a person whose sacral chakra is underactive would have a low sexual drive and a person with an overactive sacral chakra would have an excessive sexual drive. Now using that example, we can all relate to that, can we not? Surely each of us has gone though life, have we not, and found our sexual desires and needs constantly changing, even though we probably gave little thought as to why.

We have been on an amazing journey together. I hope you are enjoying it as much as I am. But it is not over. The bus has just stopped for awhile so that we, the passengers, can take a break. If you want to continue on this journey, I can begin creating our itinerary for the next leg of or journey, in my book to be called, *"The Great Tomorrow..... the Second Leg of the Journey"*.

# After Thoughts

In my forward, I said Volume One may be the only volume I ever publish..or there could be many to follow. ...I ask you to be the decision maker. Is this the end of the beginning, or the beginning of the unlimited end.

If it is the end of the beginning, I hope the information that spirit and I provided you makes a difference in your lives. I know it will in mine, and I will it read it many times over the years and in future lifetimes. Like all of my other five books, I find every time I select one to read, it is if I was reading if for the first time. Is that not true of many experiences we have in life, although we may have had that same experience before?

Yesterday I was playing Texas Poker (actually playing Omaha) with six of my friends. I told them during a pause in the game (I had the cards and was the dealer, so I controlled the pause)....:"Gentleman, I have news for you. I am having a dream right now, and every one of you are a figment of my imagination. When I wake up, you will no longer exist".

One of them answered, "Nick, what if it is me that is having the dream, and not you?" And I responded that he was exactly right; that every one of them is having a dream, and we only exist for one another until we wake up from our dream... (have our soul's transition).

But is that not what life is, in reality? We have a dream that begins when we are a very little baby, coming out of our mother's womb...and we create all the characters (and experiences) in our lives. We can laugh with them, cry with them; make love with them, (be selective), love them or have disdain for them.

We can travel the world with them, or decide to delete them from our lives and have no relationship with them at all. That is your choice, every moment, every day, for life is your dream.

Have you ever been to Paris? What if Paris doesn't really exist? What if it is only your imagination that created Paris, and it is only there when you get off the plane and start seeing the sights..that you create..that you imagine exists in your imaginary Paris?

You think that is not possible? You can have four friends go to the Paris they envision, and each will tell you their own version of what they saw... and created. Parisians were hostile to Americans..Parisians love Americans....Parisians are fun loving..Parisians are uptight..etc., etc., etc.

With every experience you have, you created that experience, and it is different than any experiences anyone else has had. Don't you see, you are living in a movie; that you are writing the script of... directing... producing... and are starring in?

I don't like long AFTER THOUGHTS IN A BOOK. So I will say so long for now..see you soon..or won't I see you again? I don't know. You decide. Help me write the script.

God bless you as you continue on your journey.

Nick Bunick

# Contact the Author

When *The Messengers* came out in 1997 we provided an address for people to write to us, and we also listed phone numbers. This created a problem, for we received more than 10,000 letters in the first six months, and it was impossible to respond to everybody. Of those we did respond to, many began to write to us on a regular basis, which created an even greater logjam. My staff and I felt bad that we couldn't answer all of the mail. The same is true of the phone calls—we had four lines that were constantly jammed.

For those reasons, we've decided that instead of a mailing address and phone numbers, we would provide a Website in order for you to reach us:

### www.nickbunick.com

There will be a place for the media to click for TV and radio interview requests, talk-show invitations, and magazine and newspaper features. We will make every effort to reply to inquiries within 24 hours.

We're committed to making our world a better place to live, and to doing everything in our power to help foster universal compassion and universal love around the world. We welcome your ideas and involvement. It will take many dedicated people, but I know we can do it. As I have written, an idea of God's cannot be defeated; and we have God, Oneness, Jeshua, and our angels and spirit guides on our team.

There are many changes that must be brought about, but with your help, I know we can be successful.

Love and blessings to each of you. — **Nick Bunick**

# Other Books by Nick Bunick

**The Messengers**……..In 1997 this book took the country by storm and became an instant New York Times best seller. The authors were Gary Hardin and Nick Bunick. Nick was the subject of this amazing book that impacted the lives of over a million people.

The first half of this book tells of the incredible miracles that happened in Nick's life, which placed him on the path he is on today. The second half of this extraordinary book is the fascinating transcription of the tapes when Nick was hypnotized and taken back 2000 years ago to the lifetime of Paul………This book will have a major impact in your life…………

**In God's Truth**…..This book was written by Nick describing the amazing events in his life that happened after the publishing of *The Messengers.* It provides you the truth and evidence of the role that your angels and spirit guides play in your life. It gives you insights into the understanding of our souls, and proof as well, as the history of reincarnation. This book will help you understand your relationship with God and enhance your own spirituality as well to understand there is no such thing as death. You will experience a healing of your own spirit and soul.

**Time for Truth….A New Beginning**…...This miraculous book is destined to change your life as well as the world as we know it today. It has been written for you and everybody else on Earth who is interested in the truth and a new beginning. *This book* will take you on an incredible journey. It also presents you with the true story of what happened.

Two thousand years ago, revealing how messages of compassion and love were turned into teachings of guilt and fear. Along the way you will be given a new and profound understanding of the spiritual world and the purpose of your life. This book is the pathway to transformation and enlightenment and a new beginning.

**The Commitment**......This is an incredible book that will provide you with the details of the life of Jeshua (Jesus) and the Apostle Paul beyond anything that has ever been written before.........You will discover in this true historical novel what Jeshua and Paul looked like; what they wore; the food they ate; how they entertained themselves; what were their goals and dreams; what were their motivations.....how they dealt with the challenges in their lives... and you will experience with them the decisions they made that impacted the lives of billions of people throughout history, and even today, with miracles and pro-found channeled spiritual messages.

Made in the USA
Monee, IL
15 November 2020

47763414R00046